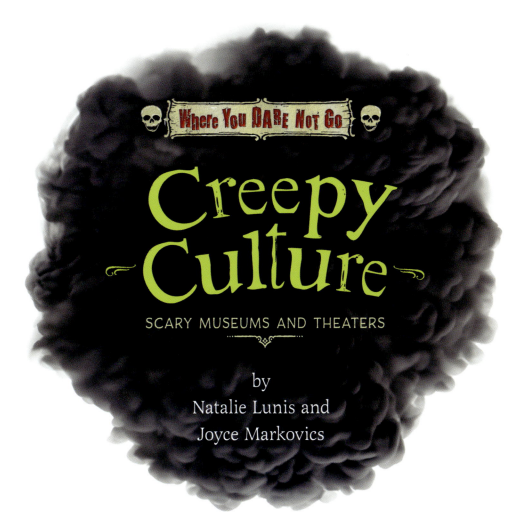

Where You DARE Not Go

Creepy Culture

SCARY MUSEUMS AND THEATERS

by
Natalie Lunis and
Joyce Markovics

Minneapolis, Minnesota

Credits

Cover, © Nasreen/Adobe Stock and © grandfailure/Adobe Stock and © Kathy/Adobe Stock and © Jakub Krechowicz/Adobe Stock and © Ruslan Gilmanshin/Adobe Stock and © Nataliya Westphal/Adobe Stock; 4–5, © AliceCam/Shutterstock and © peter_waters/Adobe Stock and © josefkubes/Adobe Stock and © Degimages/Adobe Stock; 6 © AevanStock/Shutterstock; 7TR, © Public domain/Wikimedia; 8B, © TCD/Prod.DB/Alamy Stock Photo; 8MR, © TCD/Prod.DB/Alamy Stock Photo; 9MR, © AmityPhoto/Alamy Stock Photo; 10B, © Ajay Suresh/Wikimedia; 10ML, © Public domain/Wikimedia; 11TR, © Public domain/Wikimedia; 12, © Douglas/Adobe Stock; 13TR, © Everett Collection/Shutterstock; 13BL, © ysbrandcosijn/Adobe Stock; 13BR, © Public domain/Wikimedia; 14, © Everett Collection Inc/Alamy Stock Photo; 15TR, © Everett Collection/Shutterstock; 15MR, © Public domain/Wikimedia; 15BR, © photoeverywhere/Adobe Stock; 16ML, © cowardlion/Shutterstock; 16B, © AnnaDudek/iStock Photo; 17TR, © Paul Juser/Shutterstock; 17BR, © master1305/Adobe Stock; 18, © Detroit Publishing Company Collection/Library of Congress; 19TR, © RGR Collection/Alamy Stock Photo; 19BL, © Noel/Adobe Stock; 20, © Molly Lewis/Wikimedia; 20BR, © Philip Scalia/Alamy Stock Photo; 21TR, © Michael Snell/Alamy Stock Photo; 22, © Petr Kovalenkov/Alamy Stock Photo; 23TR, © Maximum Film/Alamy Stock Photo; 24, © Ham/Wikimedia; 25BR, © Public domain/Wikimedia; 26, © Louis Berk/Alamy Stock Photo; 27BR, © Chronicle/Alamy Stock Photo; 28, © Diane Modafferi/Alamy Stock Photo; 29TR, © Public domain/Wikimedia; 29BL, © John Mosbaugh/Wikimedia; 30, © William Barton/Shutterstock; 31TL, © TIllustrated London News/Mary Evans Picture Library; 32B, © Portland Press Herald/Getty Images; 32L, © Paul Juser/Shutterstock; 33TR, © Randy Duchaine/Alamy Stock Photo; 34, © Lee Foster/Alamy Stock Photo; 35TR, © ullstein bild/ Getty Images; 36, © Public domain/Wikimedia; 37TR, © Maurice Savage/Alamy Stock Photo; 37BL, © Carito Caracol/Adobe Stock; 38, © BrianScantlebury/iStock Photo; 39TR, © Chuck Pefley/Alamy Stock Photo; 40, © f11photo/Adobe Stock; 41TR, © Public domain/Wikimedia; 41BL, © Lakeview Images/Shutterstock; 42–43, © maodoltee/Shutterstock

Bearport Publishing Company Product Development Team

Publisher: Jen Jenson; Director of Product Development: Spencer Brinker; Managing Editor: Allison Juda; Editor: Cole Nelson; Associate Editor: Naomi Reich; Associate Editor: Tiana Tran; Designer: Kim Jones; Designer: Kayla Eggert; Designer: Steve Scheluchin; Production Specialist: Owen Hamlin

Statement on Usage of Generative Artificial Intelligence

Bearport Publishing remains committed to publishing high-quality nonfiction books. Therefore, we restrict the use of generative AI to ensure accuracy of all text and visual components pertaining to a book's subject. See BearportPublishing.com for details.

Library of Congress Cataloging-in-Publication Data is available at www.loc.gov or upon request from the publisher.

ISBN: 979-8-89577-091-7 (hardcover)
ISBN: 979-8-89577-208-9 (ebook)

Copyright © 2026 Bearport Publishing Company. All rights reserved. No part of this publication may be reproduced in whole or in part, stored in any retrieval system, or transmitted in any form or by any means, electronic, mechanical, photocopying, recording, or otherwise, without written permission from the publisher. Bearport Publishing is a division of FlutterBee Education Group.

For more information, write to Bearport Publishing, 5357 Penn Avenue South, Minneapolis, MN 55419.

Contents

Eerily Artistic 4

Lincoln's Murder Lives On 6

The Devil Doll 8

A Curse Strikes Again 10

Dead Ringer. 12

Playing the Palace 14

The Spooky Staircase 16

"Good Night, Olive!" 18

Curious and Creepy 20

The Phantom of the Opera 22

The Cursed Coffin 24

The Man in Gray 26

Viewers, Beware! 28

The Strangler Jacket 30

Truth—or Fiction? 32

On with the Show! 34

Cries and Dark Shadows 36

The Boy in the Balcony. 38

The Bloody Butcher 40

A World of . . . Creepy Culture 42

Glossary 44

Read More 46

Learn More Online 46

Index. 47

Eerily Artistic

Millions of people visit museums and go to theaters each year. Seeing spectacular artworks and stunning live performances can be a thrilling experience. But what happens if you begin to see beings that are no longer alive? How would you react if you found yourself in a spooky building filled with objects from murders, mysteries, or haunted happenings? Exposing yourself to culture is usually a good thing . . . until things start getting creepy!

Lincoln's Murder Lives On

FORD'S THEATRE
WASHINGTON, D.C.

People expect to see a tragedy acted out on the stage of a theater. About 150 years ago, however, people at a theater in Washington, D.C., witnessed something truly terrible take place in the audience during a production. In fact, the event turned out to be one of the greatest tragedies in American history.

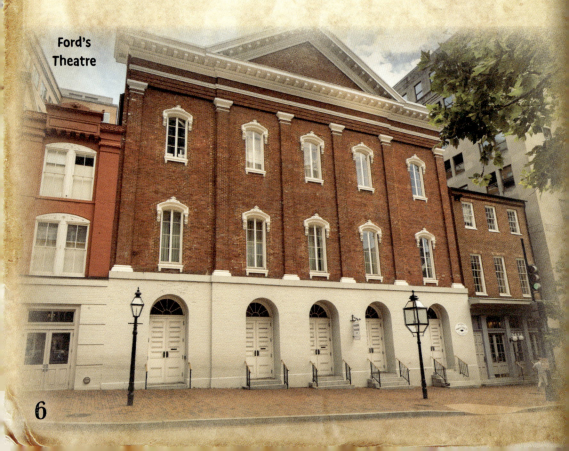

Ford's Theatre

On the night of April 14, 1865, President Abraham Lincoln was watching a play in Ford's Theatre with his wife, Mary, next to him. Around 10:15 p.m., a shot rang out. A man named John Wilkes Booth had just fired a gun at the president. A Southerner, Booth was acting in revenge. He blamed Lincoln for the defeat of the South in the U.S. Civil War (1861–1865).

An illustration of the assassination of Abraham Lincoln

Lincoln died the next morning, and Ford's Theatre remained closed for more than 100 years. Since its reopening in 1968, some people have claimed to see a ghostly version of Lincoln's assassination acted out. Audience members say they have heard footsteps rushing to the area where Lincoln sat, followed by a gunshot and screams. Mary has been seen pointing at the stage, which Booth crossed as he made his escape. She cries out, "He has killed the president!" Onstage, Booth has sometimes been seen running away. Some actors have felt an icy chill—perhaps a sign that Booth's spirit still lurks in the theater's shadows.

Today, part of Ford's Theatre is a museum. People who visit can see objects related to Lincoln's presidency and his assassination. Among them are the clothes Lincoln wore the night he was shot and the gun John Wilkes Booth used.

The Devil Doll

WARRENS' OCCULT MUSEUM
MONROE, CONNECTICUT

This small museum was truly the stuff of nightmares. Among its haunted treasures were children's tombstones and a mirror said to be able to summon spirits. The centerpiece of the collection was a wicked doll.

Lorraine and Ed Warren

Warrens' Occult Museum

For more than 60 years, this museum contained the personal collection of Ed and Lorraine Warren. For decades, the Warrens worked as ghost hunters. During that time, they investigated more than 10,000 spooky cases and collected many of the creepy items they found. The Warrens housed their collection in the basement of their own home in Connecticut.

One of the Warrens' most prized objects was a grinning doll called Annabelle. The rag doll once belonged to a woman named Donna, who claimed it would move mysteriously around her apartment. It also left creepy handwritten messages, including a note that read, "Help us." One night, the rag doll supposedly climbed up the leg of one of Donna's friends as he was fast asleep. It then latched onto his throat and tried to strangle him! Frightened for her life, Donna contacted the Warrens. They became convinced the spirit of a dead girl named Annabelle Higgins possessed the doll. The couple took the doll and placed it in their museum.

Annabelle, the doll

Visitors to the Warrens' Occult Museum could view Annabelle in a glass box. A sign warned people to absolutely not open the case . . . or else!

The Warrens' museum opened in 1952. It closed after Ed and Lorraine passed away, shuttering its doors for good in 2019.

9

A Curse Strikes Again

THE LONGACRE THEATRE
NEW YORK CITY, NEW YORK

The Boston Red Sox play baseball far away from New York's famous Broadway theaters. So how could a curse on Boston's baseball team also bring bad luck to one of these showplaces? The answer has to do with a business deal that took place more than 100 years ago.

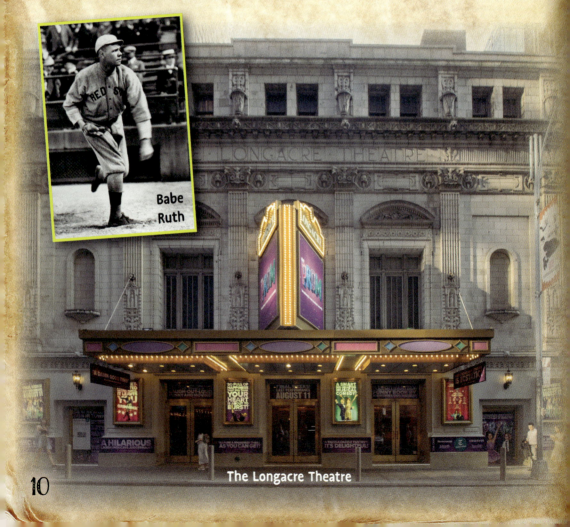

Babe Ruth

The Longacre Theatre

In the early part of the 1900s, Harry Frazee was a successful businessman. He was involved in many deals, including the building of the Longacre Theatre in New York City.

Harry Frazee

At first, this large theater was home to a series of hits. Later, however, it struggled. Sometimes it stood empty, with no plays onstage and no people in the audience. At other times, plays were put on, but the flops outnumbered the successes.

Is there an explanation for the theater's lack of success? Some people think so. They point out that in 1919, Harry Frazee—who also owned the Boston Red Sox—sold one of its star players, Babe Ruth, to the New York Yankees. Ruth, who was nicknamed the Bambino, went on to become one of the greatest home run hitters in the history of baseball. Shortly after he was sold to the Yankees, the Red Sox began a long losing streak. Many people call this slump the curse of the Bambino, blaming Ruth's sale for the misfortune. Because Harry Frazee also owned the Longacre Theatre, some think the theater's losing streak was related to the curse as well.

After losing Babe Ruth to the Yankees in 1919, the Red Sox did not win any World Series championships until 2004. The Yankees, on the other hand, have won more than 25 championships since adding Ruth.

Dead Ringer

CLEVELAND MUSEUM OF ART
CLEVELAND, OHIO

Within this historic museum are priceless works of art by famous artists such as Pablo Picasso and Claude Monet. Visitors enjoy gazing at the masterpieces. Who—or what—else might be looking at the art? The answer will send shivers down your spine.

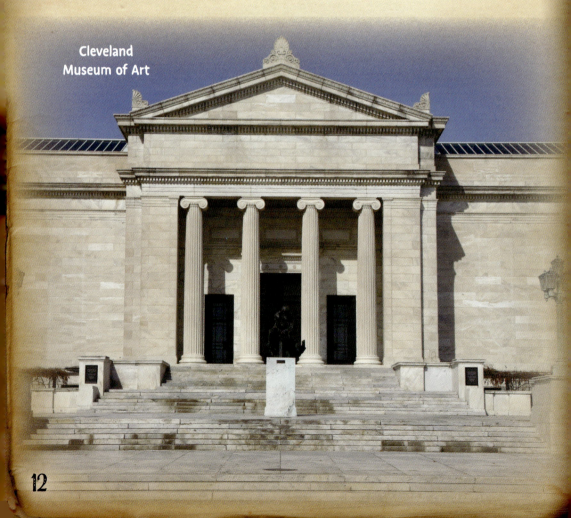

Cleveland Museum of Art

French artist Claude Monet died in 1926. He is most famous for his colorful, airy paintings, as well as his bushy white beard. In 2015, workers were putting the finishing touches on a new exhibit of Monet's art at the Cleveland Museum of Art when, suddenly, a museum staff member noticed something strange on a balcony above the gallery. "This man resembling Claude Monet was . . . peering down into the lower lobby," said the worker. He immediately snapped a photo to show others what he had seen.

Claude Monet

Many agree that the creepy person in the photo is a dead ringer for the artist Claude Monet. "What are the chances someone looks like that and happens to be at the museum the day we are finishing installation?" said another museum worker. Could it be Monet's ghost?

A former Cleveland Museum of Art director has also been spotted wandering in the oldest part of the building. He died in 1978.

A painting by Claude Monet

Playing the Palace

THE PALACE THEATRE
NEW YORK CITY, NEW YORK

Shortly after the Palace Theatre opened in 1913, just about every person in show business dreamed about performing on its stage. Today, it seems that many who managed to make it there also found it hard to leave. They were so thrilled by their successes that they continue to appear there—even after death.

The Palace Theatre

Perhaps the most chilling ghost at the Palace is that of Louis Borsalino, an acrobat who fell 18 feet (5.5 m) while walking across a tightrope. It is said that anyone who sees his spirit will die within a year!

The Palace Theatre was world-famous during the time of vaudeville—a style of entertainment in which different performers, including singers, dancers, actors, and acrobats, appeared together in a single show. After vaudeville ended in the mid-1930s, the Palace continued to be a popular place to present plays, concerts, and musicals. Since so many people have been onstage there over the years, it's not surprising that more than 100 spirits are said to haunt the building.

Harry Houdini

Some big-name performers are a part of the Palace's ghostly lineup. For example, the famous magician Harry Houdini has made his presence known to stage crews. Legendary singer and actor Judy Garland has been seen near a door that was built especially for her entrance during her concerts. Other ghosts may not be known by name, yet they are still unforgettable. They include a woman in a white gown who plays the cello in the orchestra pit, a sad-looking little girl who sits in the balcony, and a little boy who rolls a toy truck on the floor behind a row of seats.

Judy Garland

The Spooky Staircase

THE QUEEN'S HOUSE
NATIONAL MARITIME MUSEUM
GREENWICH, ENGLAND

Step inside this historic museum and former royal home to find the spiraling Tulip Stairs. This grand staircase has a flowery iron railing and twists all the way up to the top floor. Curiously, the staircase is a favorite spot for spirits.

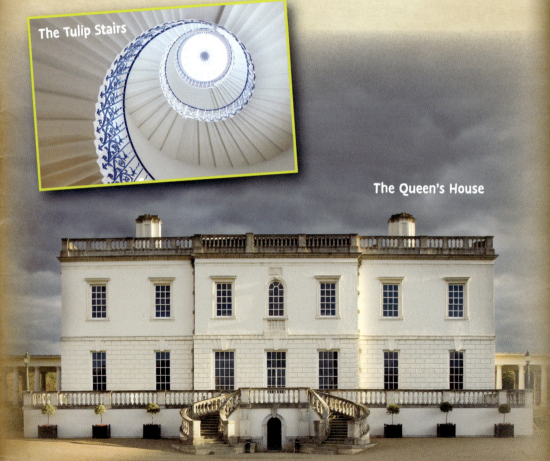

The Tulip Stairs

The Queen's House

In 1966, a visitor to the museum, the Reverend Ralph Hardy of White Rock, British Columbia, snapped a picture of the elegant staircase. When he returned home and developed the film, he was shocked at what he saw. The photo revealed two shrouded figures pulling themselves up the railing of the stairs with their hands. What had Reverend Hardy captured in the picture? To this day, no one is quite sure.

Rev. Ralph Hardy's photo showing two ghostly figures

The photo isn't the only evidence of ghostly goings-on in the museum. In 2002, a worker saw a figure wearing an old-fashioned gray dress. "I went very cold, and the hair on my arms and my neck stood on end," the worker said. Then, the figure passed right through a wall. Mysterious footsteps and the sound of children chanting have also been heard in the stairwell.

The Queen's House was built between 1616 and 1635. Previously used as a royal residence, today it is an art museum.

"Good Night, Olive!"

THE NEW AMSTERDAM THEATRE
NEW YORK CITY, NEW YORK

In the 1990s, the New Amsterdam Theatre was being repaired after standing dark and empty for a few years. During this time, a night watchman at the theater saw a shocking sight. A beautiful woman in a green dress suddenly appeared—and then disappeared by walking through a brick wall. Who was this woman, and why was she there?

The New Amsterdam Theatre

Olive Thomas moved from her home in Pennsylvania to New York City in 1913, hoping for fame and fortune. She found both a few years later on the stage of the New Amsterdam Theatre. There, she performed as a showgirl in the *Ziegfeld Follies*, a show known for its hit tunes and talented dancers.

Showgirl Olive Thomas

Olive's glittering life came to an early end, however. One night in 1920, while she was on a trip to Paris with her new husband, Jack Pickford, she felt restless. Thinking that it would help her fall asleep, she took some powerful medication from a blue bottle that belonged to Jack. Tragically, the medicine killed her instead.

Shortly after her death, Olive began appearing once again at the New Amsterdam—this time, as a ghost. She is almost always seen wearing a beautiful green beaded dress from her days in the Follies. In her hand, she carries a blue bottle.

Because Olive is so well known to those who work at the New Amsterdam, the theater's owners have hung two pictures of her backstage. Each time actors pass them while leaving the theater, they make sure to say, "Good night, Olive!"

19

Curious and Creepy

MÜTTER MUSEUM
PHILADELPHIA, PENNSYLVANIA

At the Mütter Museum, visitors enter a large room filled with hundreds of glass cases. When they look closer, they come face to face with curiosities beyond imagination.

Mütter Museum

This museum got its name from Dr. Thomas Dent Mütter, a Philadelphia surgeon who died in 1859. He had devoted his life to helping others—and to collecting some very unusual things. In addition to medical tools, Dr. Mütter collected human bones and tumors from his patients. In all, he acquired 1,700 odd medical items, and he used them to create a museum.

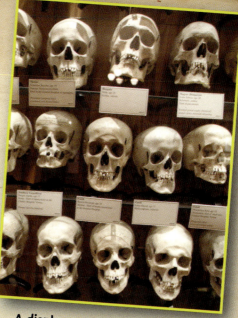

A display at the Mütter Museum

Today, more than 37,000 objects are housed at the Mütter Museum. One of the most interesting pieces is a book bound in human skin! A particularly shocking collection in the museum is made up of 2,374 objects that had been removed from people's throats and airways. These include coins, toys, and buttons. There is also a series of slides that displays actual slices of brain tissue. One of the tissue samples came from the brain of the famous scientist Albert Einstein!

The Mütter Museum first opened its doors to visitors in 1863, and it has been dedicated to medical history and science ever since.

21

The Phantom of the Opera

PALAIS GARNIER
PARIS, FRANCE

Built in the late 1800s, the Palais Garnier is one of the most beautiful theaters in the world and home to the Paris Opera. It is also the setting for one of the world's most famous horror stories—*The Phantom of the Opera*. Since the building where the story takes place really exists, could any of the shocking events in the tale be real as well?

Palais Garnier

Written in the early 1900s, *The Phantom of the Opera* tells a tragic and frightening tale. In it, a mysterious man named Erik lives in a hidden set of rooms under the magnificent Paris Opera. His face is horribly disfigured, so he wears a white mask to cover it. When Erik sees a beautiful young opera singer named Christine, he falls in love with her and tries to charm her by singing to her from a hiding place offstage. Later, he kidnaps Christine and takes her to his underground home, hoping she will grow to love him.

Erik from the 2004 film *The Phantom of the Opera*

The Phantom himself never existed. However, Gaston Leroux, the author of the novel, got the idea for one of its most thrilling scenes from an event that really took place at Palais Garnier in 1896. That year, a piece of equipment that helped the theater's huge chandelier stay balanced fell from the ceiling, killing someone below. In the novel, Erik causes a giant chandelier to fall onto the audience. It is during the confusion that follows that he snatches Christine from the stage.

The Phantom of the Opera novel was turned into a musical. It went on to become the longest-running musical in Broadway history.

The Cursed Coffin

THE BRITISH MUSEUM
LONDON, ENGLAND

This museum houses one of the largest collections of ancient Egyptian artifacts in the world. One of the objects is a 3,500-year-old coffin that once held the mummy of a high priestess. Many believe the coffin is cursed.

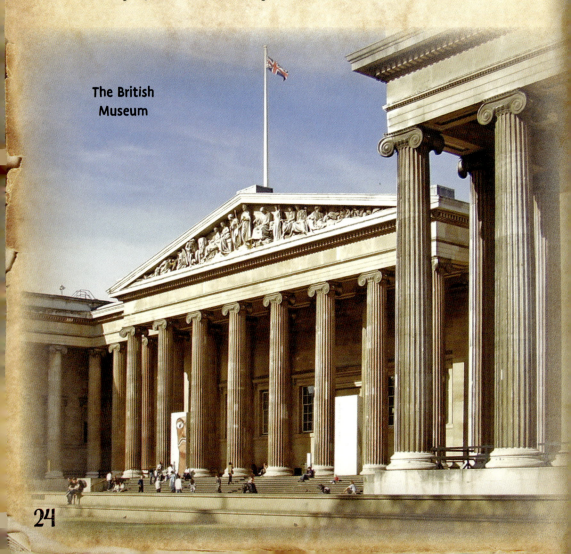

The British Museum

The tale of the mummy's curse begins in 1865. At that time, an Englishman named Thomas D. Murray was visiting Egypt. There, he purchased an ancient Egyptian coffin. A few days later, while Murray was hunting for ducks along the Nile River, he accidentally shot himself in the arm. Then, two of Murray's servants who had helped move the coffin died.

Once back in London, Murray was visited by a clairvoyant, who warned him of the coffin's evil powers. Soon after, a photographer who had taken a picture of the coffin passed away suddenly. When the photo was developed, it revealed a ghostly, terrifying face. In 1889, the coffin was brought to the British Museum. A worker who had touched the case was struck down by a deadly illness. Soon, museum cleaning crews reported that they were overcome with terror whenever they went near the mummy case. Could the coffin's curse be real?

A 1904 newspaper headline read, "Priestess dead centuries ago, still potent to slay and afflict." The headline referred to the ancient coffin Murray had found.

The Man in Gray

DRURY LANE THEATRE
LONDON, ENGLAND

People are often frightened when they see a ghost. Yet in one London theater, the actors and staff are happy to see a certain spirit known as the Man in Gray. Why is his ghostly presence so welcome?

Drury Lane Theatre

No one at Drury Lane Theatre knows for certain who the Man in Gray was during his life. According to some, he was an actor who was in love with one of the theater's actresses, and his death occurred during a fight over her.

A number of important things are known about the mysterious man's ghost, however. For example, he wears a long gray coat, a ruffled shirt, knee-length pants, and a three-cornered hat. In other words, he wears the outfit of a gentleman from the 1700s or early 1800s. He never says anything, and he always appears during rehearsals in the afternoon hours. Most important of all, since he first began appearing in the 1930s, he has been seen only before shows that turned out to be hits. For that reason, people at Drury Lane are truly thrilled to see this well-dressed ghost.

The Man in Gray is not the only spirit who haunts Drury Lane. In fact, it is known as London's most-haunted theater because so many spirits have been seen there. Among them is a famous clown named Joseph Grimaldi, who died in 1837.

An illustration of Joseph Grimaldi dressed as a clown

Viewers, Beware!

MUSEUM OF DEATH
LOS ANGELES, CALIFORNIA

With a name that says it all, this museum doesn't shy away from death. Its collection of coffins and other grisly trinkets promises to make your skin crawl.

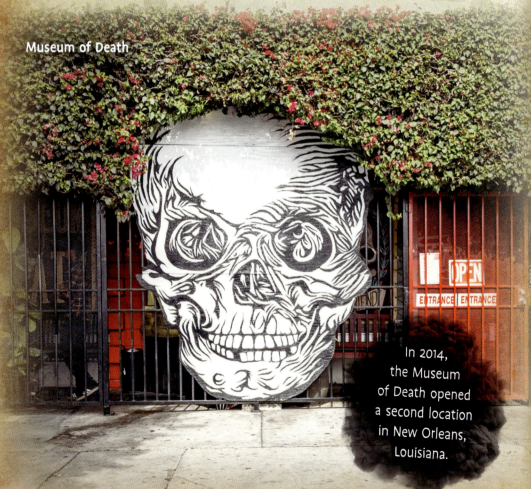

Museum of Death

In 2014, the Museum of Death opened a second location in New Orleans, Louisiana.

The Museum of Death opened in 1995 in a building that used to be a mortuary. Its first exhibit was a collection of artwork made by murderers. From there, the museum's owners gathered personal items that belonged to serial killers, including letters and drawings. Over the years, the collection grew to include everything from body bags to bloody crime-scene photos.

The serial killer Henri Landru

One of the museum's most shocking pieces is a severed head. The head belonged to serial killer Henri Désiré Landru, who was born in Paris in 1869. Landru killed 10 people between 1915 and 1919. After killing them, he burned their bodies. In 1919, he was found guilty of the murders, and in 1922, he was beheaded as punishment. Although his body was buried, his head was preserved. Today, visitors to the museum can look into the eyes of a real-life monster.

Landru's severed head

29

The Strangler Jacket

THE DUKE OF YORK'S THEATRE
LONDON, ENGLAND

Places, such as houses, theaters, and graveyards, are often said to be haunted. Can an object, such as a piece of clothing, be haunted as well? A strange event that occurred at one London theater suggests that it can.

The Duke of York's Theatre

In 1949, Thora Hird was onstage performing in a play called *The Queen Came By*. She was an experienced actor and was used to being in front of an audience, yet she felt strangely uncomfortable. It was as if the black jacket she was wearing as part of her costume was getting tighter and tighter—especially around her neck.

Thora Hird (left)

When other women who worked at the Duke of York's Theatre tried the jacket on, they had the same feeling. Reportedly, one woman even had red marks on her neck after wearing it.

What could have caused the strange tightening? According to some, years before Thora Hird's performance, the jacket had been worn by an actress who was later murdered. Even more shocking was the way she had died—being strangled to death by a jealous boyfriend.

People say that after being used as a theatrical costume, the black jacket was bought by an American man who lived in California. His wife and daughter both felt as if they were being choked when they tried the jacket on.

Truth—or Fiction?

INTERNATIONAL CRYPTOZOOLOGY MUSEUM
PORTLAND, MAINE

Does Bigfoot actually prowl secluded forests? Is the Loch Ness Monster real? The International Cryptozoology Museum might hold some clues. Visitors can look at the more than 10,000 items on display and then decide for themselves what's real and what's not.

Loren Coleman

International Cryptozoology Museum

Loren Coleman is the museum's founder and a famous cryptozoologist. Cryptozoology is the study of creatures that many people believe in, but that science has not proven to exist. Over the years, Coleman has collected everything from photos of strange beasts to casts of huge footprints. He's especially proud of the museum's hair and poop samples, which are said to belong to a Yeti.

A model of a Yeti

In folklore of the Himalayan mountain range in Asia, a Yeti is a large, hairy creature that walks on two legs. Over the years, there have been many reports of Yeti sightings. In 1925, an explorer named N. A. Tombazi spotted a large creature near Zemu Glacier. "Unquestionably, the figure in outline was exactly like a human being, walking upright," he said. "It showed up dark against the snow."

Coleman hopes that museum visitors keep an open mind. He invites people to examine the objects and consider for themselves: Could there be bizarre, still undiscovered creatures living in the world?

The museum also has a life-size model of a coelacanth (SEE-luh-kanth). This large fish was thought to be extinct—until one was found alive in 1938.

On with the Show!

OREGON SHAKESPEARE FESTIVAL
ASHLAND, OREGON

According to a famous show business saying, the show must go on. That's certainly true at an outdoor theater in Oregon. Here, one actor seems to feel that nothing should keep him off the stage—not even his own death.

The outdoor theater at the Oregon Shakespeare Festival

Today, Charles Laughton is best known as a movie actor. In 1933, he won an Academy Award for playing an English king in *The Private Life of Henry VIII*. In 1939, he starred as a frightening-looking bell ringer in *The Hunchback of Notre Dame*.

Charles Laughton in *The Private Life of Henry VIII*

Charles Laughton, however, began his acting career onstage in England and continued to appear in plays even after becoming famous in Hollywood. He especially loved acting in the works of famous English playwright William Shakespeare. As a result, he gladly accepted an offer to play the title role in *King Lear*—one of Shakespeare's greatest tragedies—at the Oregon Shakespeare Festival.

The role became more tragic and unforgettable than anyone could have imagined, however. Laughton died in December 1962, a few months before the play's scheduled opening. When the play did go on with another actor, people heard a strange moaning sound. It moved from the back of the audience and onto the stage. Next, a cold wind blew toward the stage, knocking the actors' hats off. Had Charles Laughton made it to opening night after all?

Since its first appearance at the Oregon Shakespeare Festival, Laughton's ghost has been heard moaning many times and has sometimes even been seen. The ghost is said to be especially active when *King Lear* is being performed.

Cries and Dark Shadows

THACKRAY MUSEUM OF MEDICINE
LEEDS, ENGLAND

Shhh . . . did you hear that? It's best not to enter this museum at night. Despite its grand exterior, the building has a frightful past. It's a place where the dead are very much alive.

Thackray Museum of Medicine

The museum has large displays that show what life was like in the 1800s. One exhibit, entitled "Pain, Pus, and Blood," describes surgery before anesthesia. Another display is devoted to the Yorkshire Witch, whose real name was Mary Bateman. Mary was a thief who tricked people into believing she had magical powers. In 1806, she poisoned a woman after promising to help her, and a few years later, Mary was executed for her crimes. For years, her skeleton hung on display at the museum. After her death, strips of Mary's skin were dried and sold as magic charms.

A box of medical tools from the 1800s

In addition to learning all about the spooky exhibits, museum visitors have also had some ghostly encounters. Some people say they have been grabbed by unseen hands, while reports of darting shadows and whimpering voices are also common. Is this museum creepy or cool? You be the judge.

The building that houses the museum opened in 1861 as the Leeds Union Workhouse, where very poor people lived and worked. Later, it was a hospital. In 1997, the building became the medical museum.

The Boy in the Balcony

THE KIMO THEATRE
ALBUQUERQUE, NEW MEXICO

Built in 1927, the KiMo Theatre is known for its beautiful and unusual design. Inside, the theater, artwork was created to remind audiences of the area's Native American culture, including nine large murals showing scenes from the American Southwest. The stunning decor is not all the theater is famous for, however. It is also the place where the ghost of a boy chooses to spend his days—just as he did during his short but happy life.

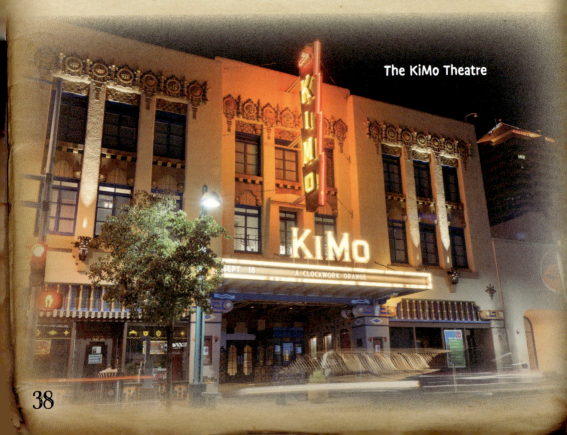

The KiMo Theatre

When the KiMo opened, movies were becoming a popular form of entertainment. As a result, the theater's owners decided that it would be a place for people to see films as well as theater performances.

By the beginning of the 1950s, movies were still a big attraction at the KiMo. Six-year-old Bobby Darnall gladly spent many hours watching them from the theater's beautiful balcony. One day, however, a horrible accident occurred. A boiler exploded, injuring seven people in the lobby and killing Bobby Darnall. Sadly, he had left his seat in the balcony to go downstairs.

Inside the KiMo Theatre

In the years afterward, the little boy has been seen in the theater many times. He has also been known to play tricks, such as tripping actors onstage or causing lights to go out. For this reason, workers at the KiMo began leaving little gifts and treats, such as doughnuts, out for him. Their offerings seem to have worked. Bobby has become known as a slightly mischievous but mostly friendly ghost.

The KiMo's name—which means mountain lion—is a blend of two words from the local Tewa language.

The Bloody Butcher

THE LOUVRE
PARIS, FRANCE

Each year, millions of people go to the Louvre museum in France to see its huge art collection. Yet the museum holds more than just priceless art. Once described as the most haunted place in Paris, the Louvre is best for art lovers who aren't afraid of ghosts.

The Louvre museum

Some people believe the Louvre holds artworks painted with human blood!

Parts of the Louvre date back to 1190, when it was used as a fortress and prison. In the late 1500s, it was also the site of the bloody St. Bartholomew's Day Massacre. The massacre began in 1572 after a series of killings involving French leaders. As many as 30,000 people were slaughtered in the streets.

A detail of a painting of the St. Bartholomew's Day Massacre

It's no surprise that ghostly visitors linger at the museum. There have been sightings of old prison guards, as well as the Red Man of the Tuileries—a 16th-century murderer. Also known as John the Skinner, the man worked as a butcher during his life. It's said that the Queen of France ordered him to kill her enemies. Then, the queen decided to kill John by having his throat slashed. Before he died, John said, "I will be back." Since that time, a blood-soaked man has been spotted haunting the Louvre.

41

A World of . . .

A ghostly painter in Cleveland, Ohio

A baseball curse in New York City, New York

A devil doll in Monroe, Connecticut

A tragic ending in Ashland, Oregon

A home for cryptids in Portland, Maine

A phantom boy in Albuquerque, New Mexico

Horrific vaudeville in New York City, New York

A severed head in Los Angeles, California

A lone dancer in New York City, New York

NORTH AMERICA

A historic assassination in Washington, D.C.

A creepy museum in Philadelphia, Pennsylvania

ATLANTIC OCEAN

SOUTH AMERICA

PACIFIC OCEAN

SOUTHERN OCEAN

42

Creepy Culture

Glossary

Academy Award an important award given every year to actors, directors, and others in the movie industry

afflict to cause pain or harm to someone else

anesthesia a drug given to people to put them to sleep and prevent them from feeling any pain

artifacts objects of historical interest made by people

assassination the killing of a famous or politically important person

casts objects made by shaping liquid materials in molds

charms things worn for protection

Civil War the U.S. war between the southern states and the northern states, which lasted from 1861 to 1865

clairvoyant a person said to be able to communicate with dead people

cryptids creatures that many believe in but that science has not proved to exist

curiosities things that are unusual and interesting

curse something that brings or causes evil or misfortune

dead ringer a person or thing that closely resembles another

decor the style and layout of interior furnishings

disfigured changed or ruined by injury or some other cause

embroidered decorated with designs that have been sewn in

executed put to death

extinct no longer existing; died out

flops theater productions that are failures

folklore the traditional beliefs, stories, and customs of a people

grisly causing horror or fear

hits theater productions that are successes

lobby a large room at the front of a building where people wait to enter the main part of the building

massacre the violent killing of many people

mischievous able to cause trouble, often through playful behavior

mortuary a place where dead bodies are kept

murals paintings that cover walls

orchestra pit the area that is in front of and slightly below the stage and is where musicians sit

possessed controlled by a spirit

potent very strong; powerful

priestess a woman who leads or performs religious ceremonies

rehearsals practice times for performances

royal having to do with or belonging to a king or queen

saliva a clear liquid produced in the mouths of humans and many animals

secluded hidden from view; placed apart from other people

serial killers people who murder more than one person

severed removed by cutting

shrine a place or object people visit because it's connected with someone important

shrouded hidden by a cloth or other covering

slaughtered violently killed

spirits supernatural beings, such as ghosts

summon to order someone or something to appear

surgeon a doctor who performs operations

Tewa a Native American people who live in what is now New Mexico

tissue a grouping of a particular type of cell in a body

tragedies plays with unhappy endings

tumors unusual lumps or growths in the body

vaudeville a style of entertainment that was popular in the United States from the 1880s to the early 1930s and featured a variety of acts in each show

Read More

Blohm, Craig E. *Ghost Tales and Hauntings.* San Deigo, CA: ReferencePoint Press, Inc., 2025.

Daniels, Ruby. *The Science of Ghosts (Xtreme Horror Lab).* Minneapolis: Abdo Publishing, 2024.

Lunis, Natalie and Troy Taylor. *Eerie Education: Scary Schools and Libraries (Where You Dare Not Go).* Minneapolis: Bearport Publishing Company, 2025.

Learn More Online

1. Go to **FactSurfer.com** or scan the QR code below.

2. Enter "**Creepy Culture**" into the search box.

3. Click on the cover of this book to see a list of websites.

46

Index

anesthesia 37
Bateman, Mary 37
Booth, John Wilkes 7
Borsalino, Louis 14
Boston Red Sox 10-11
British Museum, the 24-25
Civil War 7
clairvoyant 25
Cleveland Museum of Art 12-13
Coleman, Loren 32-33
Darnall, Bobby 39
Drury Lane Theatre 26-27
Duke of York's Theatre 30-31
Einstein, Albert 21
Ford's Theatre 6-7
Frazee, Harry 11
Garland, Judy 15
Grimaldi, Joseph 27
Hardy, Reverend Ralph 17
Higgins, Annabelle 9
Himalaya Mountains 33
Hird, Thora 31
Houdini, Harry 15
International Cryptozoology
    Museum 32
John the Skinner 41
KiMo Theatre 38-39
Landru, Henri Désiré 29
Laughton, Charles 35
Leroux, Gaston 23
Lincoln, Abraham 6-7
Longacre Theatre 10-11
Louvre, the 40-41

Monet, Claude 12-13
mortuary 29
Murray, Thomas D. 25
Museum of Death 28-29
Mütter, Dr. Thomas Dent 20-21
Mütter Museum 20-21
New Amsterdam Theatre 18-19
New York Yankees 11
Nile River 25
Oregon Shakespeare
    Festival 34-35
Palace Theatre 14-15
Paris Opera 22-23
Phantom of the Opera 22-23
Picasso, Pablo 12
priestess 24, 43
Queen's House, National
    Maritime Museum 16-17
Ruth, Babe 10-11
serial killer 29
Shakespeare, William 34-35
St. Bartholomew's Day
    Massacre 41
surgeon 21
Thackray Museum of
    Medicine 36-37
Thomas, Olive 19
Tombazi, N. A. 33
Tulip Stairs 16
Warrens' Occult Museum 8-9
Yeti 33
Yorkshire Witch 37

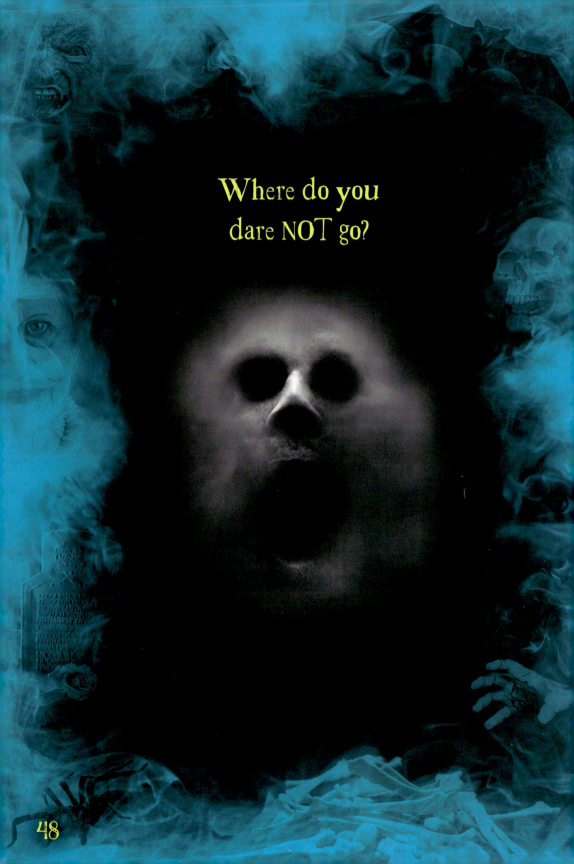